This Book Presented to

_____

From

_____

Date

_____

Trust in the LORD *with all your heart,*
And lean not on your own understanding;
In all your ways acknowledge Him,
And He shall direct your paths.
                              —Proverbs 3:5–6

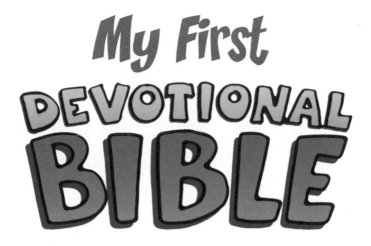

My First DEVOTIONAL BIBLE

Andy Holmes

Illustrated by Rob Suggs

Tommy NELSON®

A Division of Thomas Nelson Publishers
Since 1798

www.thomasnelson.com

My First Devotional Bible

Copyright © 2007 by Educational Publishing Concepts, Inc., Wheaton, IL.
Illustrations by Rob Suggs.
All rights reserved. No portion of this book may be reproduced in any form without the written permission of the publisher, with the exception of brief excerpts in reviews.
Published in Nashville, Tennessee, by Tommy Nelson®, a Division of Thomas Nelson®, Inc.
Visit us on the Web at www.tommynelson.com.
Tommy Nelson® books may be purchased in bulk for educational, business, fund-raising, or sales promotional use. For information, please email SpecialMarkets@ThomasNelson.com.
Scripture quotations in this book are from the *Holy Bible, New King James Version*.
Copyright © 1979, 1980, 1982 by Thomas Nelson, Inc. (Editor's note: We have retained the italic type in the *New King James Version* Bible text quoted in this book. Italic type indicates words that are not found in the original languages but are needed for clarity in English.)

Library of Congress Cataloging-in-Publication Data
  My first devotional Bible / Andy Holmes
      p. cm.
  ISBN-13: 978-1-4003-0908-5 (hardback)
  ISBN-10 1-4003-0908-5
  1. Bible stories, English. 2. Bible—Devotional use—Juvenile literature. I. Title
BS551.3.H655 2007
242'.62—dc22
                              2006029383

Printed in China
07 08 09 10 11 LEO 5 4 3 2 1

Contents

A Note from the Author

According to FunTrivia.com, there are 593,493 words in the Old Testament and 181,253 words in the New Testament, bringing the total words in the Bible to 774,746. That's a lot of words! *More than that, the Bible is filled with life-changing words.*

My First Devotional Bible will help you see what these words can mean for your life. Perhaps you've met some of these Bible characters in *My First Study Bible*; if so, now's your chance to get to know them even better. Each of the 65 devotionals in this book is designed to help you learn more about the Bible and have some fun along the way:

1. Get to know Bible characters who walked with God long before you or I walked at all.
2. Discover ways to apply what you learn from each story to your own life.
3. Read and memorize key Bible verses.
4. Explore the Bible to learn interesting facts, mysteries, and things to ponder.
5. Acquire fascinating bits of information to share with others.
6. Sharpen your Bible skills as you answer challenging questions.

So why are you still hanging around on this page? Turn the page and start the fun!

—Andy Holmes

Who's Really in Charge Here?

Genesis 2:18–3:24

I'm Adam. And I'm Eve. The first people ever. You know our story. God said we could eat anything in the garden, except one thing. God said, "Don't eat from the tree of the knowledge of good and evil." But we did anyway.

We wanted to make up our own minds about things. Take charge of our own lives. So we disobeyed. Boy, that was a mistake!

Truth is, you have to answer that same question: Who's in charge of *your* life? Like us, you'll have to answer that question every day. Will you do what you want to do? Or will you obey God?

Who? Me?

Will you do what God wants you to do even when it's not what you want to do? God builds your faith with each such challenge. Say, "Yes, Lord!" and your faith grows stronger. Say, "No, Lord," and your faith grows weaker.

BIBLE VERSE

"Therefore you shall keep the commandments of the LORD your God, to walk in His ways and to fear Him."
—*Deuteronomy 8:6*

Water, please?

When was the first sprinkler system invented?
Answer: Before man was created.

Read all about it in Genesis 2:4–6.

Did You Know?

Adam lived to be 930 years old. Picture the candles on his last birthday cake!

Challenge

What were two of the first things Adam and Eve did after they disobeyed God?

Read Genesis 3:7–8.

Sink or Swim

Genesis 6:11–7:18

Hi, ya! Captain Noah here!

No doubt you know my story by heart. "Build a big boat, Noah!" God told me. A big *what*? I wondered. So God told me exactly how to do it. It was a pretty tall order, er, so to speak, and, buoy oh buoy (Get it? That's boat humor!), did I get some strange looks from the neighbors—especially when those two skunks arrived!

Big jobs take big *stick-to-it-iveness*. Sure, I wanted to quit along the way—but I figured I had better do it with all that water coming! And I'm so glad I did. Quitters never finish anything. God needs people who'll stick with it until the task is done. God calls it *perseverance*. And it's a great thing to develop in yourself.

Who? Me?

Finish your tasks. Homework? Get it done without complaining or having to be scolded. Household chores? Do them with a smile. When you make yourself stick with these little things, you're training yourself to be able to stick with bigger things.

BIBLE VERSE

And Noah did according to all that the LORD commanded him.

—*Genesis 7:5*

Bible mystery

What was Noah's wife's name? The Bible doesn't say. Two best guesses, according to Bible scholars, are Naamah or Emzara.

Did You Know?

Animal facts:

- A rat can last longer without water than a camel.
- An ostrich's eye is bigger than its brain.
- All polar bears are left-handed.

Challenge

How many humans went aboard the ark?

Read Genesis 8:18 and 9:18.

All or Nothing

Genesis 21:1–7; 22:1–19

Hi, I'm Abraham.

Do you remember what God told me to do with my only son, Isaac? God told me to sacrifice him on an altar. Whoa! Thankfully, this is no ordinary request. As hard as it was, I obeyed. And God stopped me just in time. I was so relieved!

Here's the point: God wanted to know if I loved Him more than anything else— even more than I loved my precious son.

Guess what? God wants us to love Him most of all.

Who? Me?

When you love someone, it shows. Do three things today that show you love God. Here are some ideas: pray, treat others with kindness, tell someone about God's goodness, honor your parents.

BIBLE VERSE

But the Angel of the LORD called to him from heaven and said, "Abraham, Abraham!" So he said, "Here I am." And He said, "Do not lay your hand on the lad, or do anything to him; for now I know that you fear God, since you have not withheld your son, your only *son*, from Me."*

—*Genesis 22:11–12*

*Italics set as in NKJV. See editor's note on page 2.

Stargazing facts . . .

When God told Abraham to "look up and count the stars," he would've been there a long time. Astronomers estimate that there are 100 billion stars in our own galaxy, according to *It Couldn't Just Happen* by Lawrence O. Richards.**

** Published by Tommy Nelson™, a Division of Thomas Nelson, Inc.

Did You Know?

Abraham was Jacob and Esau's grandfather.
Read Genesis 25:19–26.

Challenge

How old was Abraham when his son Isaac was born?

Read Genesis 21:5.

Hang in There

Genesis 37:14–28; 42:1–45:5

Hi, I'm Joseph.

That's right, the guy whose father made him the colorful coat. You might recall that my brothers weren't too happy about that. In fact, they threw me into a well. Then they sold me. I became a slave, was lied about, was thrown into jail, and finally became the second most powerful man in Egypt. Wild, huh?

God can use the worst of things to bring about the best of things. So don't get discouraged when things aren't going the way you want. Hang in there. It just *seems* like forever.

Believe me, God has a plan for your life. Every day another page in God's story for you is written. Your job in every situation is to choose the right attitude.

Who? Me?

Pretend you're being observed by a news reporter from heaven. What would the reporter write about your attitudes? Every day make good choices so you are proud of the article being written about you.

BIBLE VERSE

"But as for you, you meant evil against me; *but* God meant it for good, in order to bring it about as *it is* this day, to save many people alive."

—*Genesis 50:20*

In too deep?

Some scholars think the well Joseph was thrown into might have been as deep as 40 feet. Ouch!

Did You Know?

Like Daniel, Joseph explained the meaning of dreams.

Read Genesis 40–41.

Challenge

How many brothers did Joseph have?

Read Genesis 42:3–4, carefully.

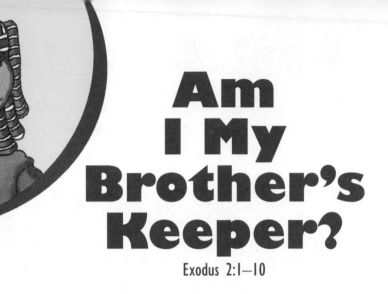

Am I My Brother's Keeper?

Exodus 2:1–10

Hi, I'm Miriam.

Do you know who my famous brother is? I'll give you a hint: He floated down the river in a basket. You guessed it! Moses!

My mother made a basket, put him in it, and I kept an eye on him as he floated down the river. *Please, God, I prayed, take care of my baby brother.* Then, when Pharaoh's daughter found him, I told her we'd take care of him for her. I had to be brave.

Being brave means being willing to do something difficult or scary. Like being a friend to someone who's being mistreated, or standing up for what's right when no one else does.

14

Who? Me?

Be a leader of good things and not a follower of bad things.

BIBLE VERSE

"Be strong and of good courage, do not fear nor be afraid of them; for the LORD your God, He *is* the One who goes with you. He will not leave you nor forsake you."

—*Deuteronomy 31:6*

God works in mysterious ways . . .

Whose face glowed so that the people were afraid of him?

Read Exodus 34:29–35.

Did You Know?

Moses tried to get God to use someone else instead of him.

Read Exodus 4:13.

Challenge

What did Moses' mother put on the basket to keep it from sinking?

Read Exodus 2:3.

Plagued with Regret

Exodus 2:11–15, 21; 7:14–12:31

Harrumph! I'm Pharaoh.

King of Egypt! The boss! All-powerful!

Well, I *thought* I was all-powerful. Turns out, I thought too highly of myself. Was I ever in for a big lesson.

"Let my people go, Pharaoh!" Moses said.

"NO!" I said. TEN TIMES! Was I foolish or what?

Turns out, I'm not the only one who lets pride get in the way. Ever feel you know better than someone else but you really don't? Ever throw a fit when things don't go your way? Take some advice from a washed-up ruler: Pride ALWAYS leads to trouble.

Who? Me?

Don't think too highly of yourself. Be confident but not too proud. Consider the needs and feelings of others.

BIBLE VERSE

When pride comes, then comes shame; but with the humble *is* wisdom.

—*Proverbs 11:2*

Papaw Moses?

Moses was 80 years old when he spoke to Pharaoh.

Read Exodus 7:7.

Did You Know?

This pharaoh is thought by many to be *Rameses II*. You can see his body for yourself in the Egyptian Museum in Cairo.

Challenge

Read about the ten plagues in Exodus 7–11. Which of the first nine do you think is the worst? Talk about it with your parent or teacher.

Do You Sea What I See?

Exodus 14:1–28

Hi, I'm Moses.

Great news! Are you ready? God can do the impossible! Trust me, I speak from personal experience.

Need an example to convince you? Here's one: I was leading God's people out of Egypt, but when we reached the Red Sea we were trapped! The sea was in front of us, and Pharaoh and his army were coming after us. There was no escaping. What were we to do?

Then God split the sea in two so we could walk across safely. Wow!

God still does the impossible (and the very hard)! Got a problem you can't seem to solve? Is something troubling you? Feel stuck in a bad situation? Tell God about it.

Who? Me?

Need help with something? God tells us to give Him our worries and to let Him help us through them.

> ### BIBLE VERSE
>
> ". . . casting all your care upon Him, for He cares for you."
>
> —1 Peter 5:7

Something fishy?

The Red Sea is a great place to go scuba diving. It is home to 200 soft and hard corals and more than 1,000 invertebrate (animals without a backbone). Some have really fun names. Here are a few: the bat star, the bloodybelly comb jelly, the fat innkeeper worm, and the hula skirt siphonophore.

Did You Know?

Moses once went without food or water for 80 days!

Read Deuteronomy 9:9–18.

Challenge

What does the name Moses mean?

Read Exodus 2:10.

Serious Respect

Leviticus 10:1–7

Hi, I'm Aaron.

I have a sad story to tell you about my sons, Nadab and Abihu.

After God had given Moses the Ten Commandments, He made my family priests to help the people honor God properly. God gave all the priests rules on how He wanted things done.

My sons, to my horror, thought that because they were priests they didn't need to follow God's rules. They were wrong. God punished them severely for not following the rules.

Looking back, two things are very clear: First, God is HOLY. That's something to think seriously about. Second, God knows our hearts.

When my sons ignored God's instructions, they showed that they had little respect for God. Think about it. Our actions and our attitudes show what we feel in our hearts.

Who? Me?

What do your actions reveal about your heart? Do your words sound harsh or grumbly? Do you make ugly faces when you are given a task to complete? Or do you talk softly and smile when you are given a task to complete?

Designer clothes . . .

The priests' garments were designed by God Himself and specially made by skilled men whom God had uniquely gifted for that purpose.

Read Exodus 28.

Did You Know?

Aaron was a good speaker. He did most of the speaking for Moses.

Read Exodus 4:14–16, 28–30.

Challenge

Was Aaron Moses' cousin, brother, or uncle?

Read Exodus 4:14.

21

Brave
Heart

Numbers 14:6–10

Hi, I'm Caleb.

I'm here to remind you to stand up for what you believe. In fact, you're going to have to if you want to follow God with all your heart.

Here's my story: Moses had led us out of slavery in Egypt, across the Red Sea (that was something to behold!), through the desert, right up to the land God had promised us. I was one of the 12 Moses told to explore the area.

It was everything I'd imagined it to be. "God has given us this land," Joshua and I told them. "Let's go in." But the other ten were full of fear. "The people there will crush us," they said. They were so afraid, they'd rather be slaves in Egypt than believe God's promise and move forward.

22

Who? Me?

Being a *light* for God means standing up for the right thing—even if you're the only one who will. Who knows: your fire might be just the spark someone else needs to stand up, too.

BIBLE VERSE

Let us hold fast the confession of *our* hope without wavering, for He who promised is faithful.

—*Hebrews 10:23*

It's all in the name . . .

Caleb's name means *bold, all heart.* And he was.

Did You Know?

Caleb risked personal harm by coming to the aid of Moses and Aaron. Why were the people in the congregation about to stone them?

Read Numbers 14:1–10.

Challenge

Which statement or phrase best describes Caleb?

Numbers 14:24;
Numbers 32:11–12;
Deuteronomy 1:36

Deuteronomy 1:36

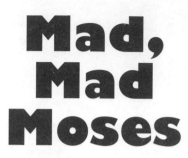

Mad, Mad Moses

Numbers 20:1–21

Hello, it's me again. Moses.

Have you ever noticed how the Bible shows people's mistakes as clearly as it shows their good behavior? Well, I've got my share of mistakes in there. One of them is not controlling my temper.

God had chosen me to lead His people out of Egypt. I did, but the people grumbled and complained all the time!

Once, God told me to gather everyone up and speak to a rock. Then He would make water flow out of it. Instead of speaking to the rock, I lost my temper and struck the rock with my rod. God was displeased with me. God still gave us the water, but He did not allow us into the Promised Land.

Who? Me?

Ever lost your temper and done something you later regretted? Hurt someone's feelings? Said something spiteful? God wants you to control your anger.

BIBLE VERSE

. . . for the wrath of man does not produce the righteousness of God.

—James 1:20

Blessed are the meek . . .

The Bible says that Moses was the most humble man on the face of the earth.

Read Numbers 12:3.

Did You Know?

Moses was also seen during Jesus' earthly life.

Read Matthew 17:1–9 and Mark 9:2–10.

Challenge

What wise advice did Moses' father-in-law give him?

Read Exodus 18:14–26.

So Long, Well Done

Deuteronomy 31–32

Hi, it's me, Moses. Last time, I promise.

I'm bidding you good-bye.

I had followed God to the best of my abilities and obeyed Him faithfully. Now, God told me my time was up. I was 120 years old. God had me walk to the top of a high mountain so I could see the land He had promised when I was in Egypt.

It was a sad-happy feeling. Sad because I wouldn't be going in. Happy because I knew I was going to be with my Lord, that I had done my best for Him, and that He was pleased.

God had chosen Joshua to lead the people now. Joshua loved God with all his heart, too. "Be strong and courageous, Joshua," I said. "God will always be with you and guide you."

Who? Me?

There are also *little good-byes*. The end of a task. The last game of the season. Even your last thought before you drift off to sleep. Will you honor God in all you do?

BIBLE VERSE

"Be strong and of good courage; do not be afraid, nor be dismayed, for the LORD your God *is* with you wherever you go."
—*Joshua 1:9*

Where is that?

The *Promised Land* or *land of Canaan* is known today as Israel.

Did You Know?

Moses had to hold his arms up all day long once.

Read Exodus 17:8–13.

Challenge

Why is Moses often called a judge?

Read Exodus 18:13–16.

Hide and Sneak

Joshua 2

Hi, I'm Rahab.

One night while I was working in my inn, I met two men who were Israelite spies.

Everyone knew God was with the Israelites. We had heard that God had freed them from slavery and opened the Red Sea when they were trapped. I wanted their God to be my God, too.

"Hide on my roof," I told them. When the king's soldiers asked me about them, I lied to keep them safe. "Promise you'll spare me and my family," I said to the spies, "just like I saved you." They promised. Then I lowered them down from my window and they escaped.

I'll let Joshua tell you about what happened to my city. Just know that God kept the spies' promise and saved my family and me from certain death.

28

Who? Me?

Rahab showed her love for God in two ways. She *believed,* and she put her belief into *action.* It isn't enough to simply *think* the right things. You have to live them out, too. Will you?

BIBLE VERSE

Likewise, was not Rahab the harlot also justified by works when she received the messengers and sent *them* out another way?

—*James 2:25*

Family matters

Rahab was King David's great-great-grandmother.

Did You Know?

Rahab was the great-grandmother of Jesus.

Challenge

What was the sign Rahab had to leave on her window in order to be saved?

Read Joshua 2:17–21.

Tall Walls Fall

Joshua 6

Hi, I'm Joshua.

God put me in charge of His people after Moses died.

One of the most famous events I had a front-row seat for was the battle of Jericho. Actually, there wasn't much of a battle at all. Truth is, God did it all. We just had to follow His clear and specific directions.

God told us to march around the city of Jericho once a day for six days. Hmm. *This isn't the battle plan I would've come up with,* I thought to myself. But, of course, *I* wasn't in charge—God was.

"On the seventh day, march around the city seven times," God added, "then have the priests blow their trumpets. When you hear the sound of the trumpet, all the people shall shout. And the wall of the city will fall down flat."

We followed God's directions carefully. And just like God said, the walls fell down.

Who? Me?

Do you follow directions well? If so, then you know the best tips for following directions well are to . . .

- Listen carefully;
- Ask questions when you don't understand; and
- Choose a good attitude.

BIBLE VERSE

Take firm hold of instruction, do not let go; keep her, for she *is* your life.
—*Proverbs 4:13*

Amazing discoveries . . .

Archaeologists have proven Jericho's destruction happened at the end of the fifteenth century BC—precisely the time when the Bible says it happened.

Did You Know?

Joshua and Jesus are basically the same name. Both are from the Hebrew *Yehoshua* or *Yeshua*. In Greek Joshua, in English Jesus—both of which mean, *he will save.*

Challenge

Did Joshua see an angel? What do you think?

Read Joshua 5:13–15.

Go! Go! Gideon

Judges 6

Hi there. I'm Gideon.

Get this—God sent an angel to tell me I was going to rescue His people from the Midianites.

But I wasn't so sure it was really God, so I asked for a sign. "Make this piece of wool wet with dew in the morning, but keep the ground around it dry." Well, He did.

Then I wanted to be extra sure. "Make the ground wet, but keep the wool dry." He did that, too!

Although thousands of men were willing to fight the Midianites, God said I'd only need 300 men! Wow!

We didn't even need to fight, because God had made the huge army of Midianites and Amalekites so scared of us that they ran off crying before we even lifted one sword.

32

Who? Me?

It takes guts to obey God's call to stand up for the weak or less fortunate or to stand up against wrong. Join in the battle for God. Think of yourself as a soldier in the Lord's army.

BIBLE VERSE

"Be strong and of good courage, and do *it;* do not fear nor be dismayed, for the LORD God— my God—*will be* with you."

—*1 Chronicles 28:20*

Incredible battle fact . . .

Gideon's 300 men defeated more than 120,000 Midianite and Amalekite swordsmen.

Read Judges 8:10.

Did You Know?

The Israelites begged Gideon and his family to be their rulers, but Gideon refused. "The Lord shall rule over you," he told them.

Read Judges 8:22–23.

Challenge

Why did Gideon offer his sacrifice to God at night?

Read Judges 6:25–27.

A Hairy Situation

Judges 16

Hey, I'm Samson, a.k.a. *Mr. Muscles*. My strength was a gift from God, but instead of protecting and treasuring that gift, I tossed it aside.

You see, I liked Delilah, but she was only trying to trick me so she could help the Philistines defeat me. She kept begging me to tell her my weakness. I knew I shouldn't, but I told her the secret about my hair. Next thing I knew, I was blind and the Philistines had put me in jail.

Much later, the evil Philistines led me to their temple to mock me. "Make us laugh, strongman," they yelled.

I asked God to make me strong once more. Then I pushed against the two pillars that held up the temple. They cracked, then crumbled, and the temple collapsed. God had heard my prayer. The Philistines were defeated.

Who? Me?

God has given you gifts, too. Has God gifted you with intelligence? Artistic talents? People skills? A great sense of humor? Use these gifts to bring glory to the Giver today.

BIBLE VERSE

For we are His workmanship, created in Christ Jesus for good works, which God prepared beforehand that we should walk in them.

—*Ephesians 2:10*

Samson vs. Lion

Samson once killed a lion with his bare hands.

Read Judges 14:6.

Did You Know?

Samson was Israel's last judge. He led Israel for 20 years.

Challenge

How many men did Samson kill using the jawbone of a donkey?

Read Judges 15:15.

First-Class Service

Ruth 1–4

Hi, I'm Ruth.

My great-grandson's name was David. Yes, *that* David. King of Israel! Giant-slayer! To think, I thought I was going to be childless.

Long before I married my husband Boaz, I lived in my home country of Moab. There was a famine in that land, and my first husband died. We didn't have any children. My mother-in-law's husband had died, too. Her name was Naomi. We were all alone.

"Go back to your family," Naomi told me, crying. But I told her, "I will stay with you. Your people will be my people, and your God will be my God."

We went to Naomi's hometown of Bethlehem. I gathered barley from nearby fields. One of the fields I worked in belonged to a man named Boaz.

Soon, Boaz met me! Then we were married and later had a son. We named him Obed. Obed had a son named Jesse. Jesse had a son named David. Yes, *that* David. God took good care of Naomi and me.

Who? Me?

Ruth's life didn't look very promising at first. Still, instead of seeking her own safety and comfort, Ruth chose to be a servant to Naomi. Do you look for ways to help others?

BIBLE VERSE

Let each of you look out not only for his own interests, but also for the interests of others.
—*Philippians 2:4*

Home, sweet home, again . . .

Boaz was Naomi's *kinsman-redeemer*, which meant he could buy back the land that once belonged to Naomi and her husband.

Did You Know?

Boaz was Rahab's son. Rahab saved the spies in Jericho.

Challenge

Naomi had two daughters-in-law. Which daughter-in-law returned to her own people?

Read Ruth 1:8–18.

Praying for a Baby

I Samuel I

Hi, my name is Hannah.

I wanted something very badly. Can you guess what it was? Riches? Fame? Beauty? No. I wanted a child, but I couldn't have one. I cried so often about it.

One day, I went to the temple to pray. "Lord," I begged God, "please let me have a baby boy. If You will do this for me, I will give him back to You. He will serve You with all his heart." Guess what? God said, "YES!" I named my baby boy Samuel. I chose that name because it means *God hears*. And yes, I kept my promise to God, too. When Samuel was still a young boy, I took him to Eli

the priest. Samuel helped Eli in the temple and grew up in the presence of the Lord.

Who? Me?

What do you do with your strong desires? God says, "Give them to Me." Do you want to be a doctor? Tell God about it. And, like Hannah, make sure you give His gifts right back to Him by using them for His glory.

BIBLE VERSE

Delight yourself also in the LORD, and He shall give you the desires of your heart.
—Psalm 37:4

Bad examples . . .

Eli's two sons, Hophni and Phinehas, were wicked. Samuel grew up around them. Instead of copying their wrong ways, Samuel chose to please God.

Did You Know?

Because Hannah kept her promise to God, God blessed her with three more sons and two daughters.

Challenge

What did Hannah make for Samuel each year?

Read 1 Samuel 2:19.

Hello?
God?

I Samuel 3

Hi, I'm Samuel.

One night when I was a young boy, I was in my bed in the temple. I heard someone calling me. "Samuel!" the voice said. I got up, walked down to Eli's room, and said, "Here I am." Eli looked confused. "I didn't call you," he told me. *That's strange*, I thought as I walked back to my room. Two more times I thought Eli had called me, but each time I was wrong.

Finally, it dawned on Eli. "God is calling you, Samuel."

I returned to my room, and God called me a fourth time. "I'm listening, Lord," I said. God told me what He was about to do and what He wanted me to do. God spoke to me other times, too. Eventually, I learned what His voice sounded like.

Who? Me?

When Samuel answered God, Samuel was ready to listen. His mouth was closed. His mind was open. His heart was eager to learn and obey. Choose this same attitude when listening to others—especially your parents and teachers.

BIBLE VERSE

"Therefore take heed how you hear. For whoever has, to him *more* will be given; and whoever does not have, even what he seems to have will be taken from him."

—*Luke 8:18*

God's footstool

Samuel was lying down near the ark of God when he heard God's voice. The ark of God was very special. It represented the actual presence of God.

Did You Know?

Samuel is thought to have been around 12 years old when this event took place.

Challenge

Learn more about the ark of God. What did it look like? (Read Exodus 25:10–22.) What was inside it? (Read Hebrews 9:4.) Was it powerful? (Read 1 Samuel 5:1–12.)

Inside/ Outside

I Samuel 16:1–13

Hi, it's me again. Samuel.

After learning what God's voice sounded like, you'd think I'd be better at figuring out what He wants. Well, you'd be wrong. But something that is always right is that God leads, we follow. Here's how God taught me that.

"Fill your horn with oil, Samuel," God told me. "Go to Jesse's house. I have chosen a new king. You must anoint him with oil." So off I went.

I met Jesse's oldest son, Eliab, first. *Ahh*, I thought, *this must be the one God has chosen. He's tall, strong, and handsome.* But God said, "This is not the man, Samuel. You're looking at the outside, but I look at a man's heart."

Abinadab was next. Then Shammah. Then the rest of Jesse's sons. "The Lord has not chosen any of these sons, Jesse," I said. "Do you have any more?" "Only my youngest, David," Jesse answered.

When young David came in, I heard God say, "Rise and anoint him, Samuel. This is the new king." So I did.

42

Who? Me?

Is it important that your friends be attractive? Rich? Dress cool? Live in a nice house? Learn to look at a person's heart instead, as God does.

BIBLE VERSE

"For *the LORD does not see* as man sees; for man looks at the outward appearance, but the LORD looks at the heart."

—*1 Samuel 16:7*

Write on, Samuel!

In addition to writing 1 and 2 Samuel, many Bible scholars think that Samuel might have written the books of Judges and Ruth, too.

Did You Know?

David is thought to have been a teenager—probably close to 15 years old—when Samuel anointed him king.

Challenge

What happened that made Samuel so sad God had to ask him, "How long will you be sad about this?"

Read 1 Samuel 15:26–16:1.

Giant Courage

1 Samuel 17

Hi, I'm David.

I was a shepherd. Now, if you're thinking being a shepherd means sitting around playing a harp and saying things like, "Here, lamby," you are mistaken. You never know when a bear, wolf, or lion might choose one of your lambs for its supper. Trust me, I know. I've had to kill a bear and a lion, and it's no picnic. However, those experiences prepared me for my most famous battle of all: Goliath.

Goliath was a skilled warrior—and he was huge! He had the whole army of Israel shaking in their sandals. "Send a man to fight me!" he roared. Nobody would. Worse still, Goliath mocked God.

"I'll fight him," I said. I picked five good stones for my slingshot and headed out. Seeing a kid challenging him really got Goliath mad. "I'll crush you, boy!" he growled. "No, Goliath," I yelled back. "This is God's fight, and you're going down!"

My aim was perfect. Goliath fell with a thud. God had honored my faith. We won the war.

44

Who? Me?

David met a big challenge with big courage. He knew he was standing up for God. Our God is still being mocked. Stand up for God when you hear others putting Him down.

BIBLE VERSE

But You, O Lord, *are* a shield for me. My glory and the One who lifts up my head.

—*Psalm 3:3*

Big news

Goliath was over 9 feet tall (maybe as tall as 10 feet 8 inches). His chest armor weighed 125 pounds. The head of his spear weighed 15 pounds.

Did You Know?

Goliath had a brother who was also very large. He was also killed in a battle. His name was Lahmi.

Read it for yourself in 1 Chronicles 20:5.

Challenge

How did Eliab, David's oldest brother, treat David when he saw him by the battlefield?

Read 1 Samuel 17:28.

A Praise Parade

2 Samuel 6:1–19

Hi, it's me again, David. Now, I'm King David.

I loved to praise God. I spent much of my time writing songs about God's power, love, and goodness. I praised Him when I was discouraged. I praised Him when I was happy.

I decided to bring the ark of God to Jerusalem—where I lived. The ark of God was very special. I gathered up 30,000 men to go with me to get the ark and bring it back. We built a new cart and put the ark of God on it.

It was a huge celebration. All of us were singing songs with all our might. We played harps, lyres, tambourines, sistrums, and cymbals! I was so excited, I danced harder than I'd ever danced before.

We put the ark of God inside the special tent I had made for it. "Everyone should praise God!" I told my people. "Make up new songs about Him! Tell Him how wonderful He is! Thank Him for all that He has done!"

Who? Me?

Praising God is more than simply singing hymns at church. Praising God means we show Him with our words, actions, bodies, talents, and energy that He is totally awesome! Praise God today.

BIBLE VERSE

Praise the LORD! For *it is* good to sing praises to our God; for *it is* pleasant, *and* praise is beautiful.

—*Psalm 147:1*

Handle with care

God was very serious about how the ark of God was to be treated. It had to be carried a certain way and could only be carried by the Levites.

Did You Know?

David left the ark of God in another city for three months before bringing it into Jerusalem.

Read why in 2 Samuel 6:6–11.

Challenge

What did David give his people after he blessed them in the name of the Lord Almighty?

Read 2 Samuel 6:18–19.

A Wise Request

I Kings 3:1–15

Hi, my name is Solomon.

My dad's name was David. He was the king for forty years. I became king next. God appeared in one of my dreams and said, "Solomon, ask for whatever you would like Me to give you." I thought for a moment, then answered, "Lord, I am so young. I will need so much wisdom to be a good king for Your people. Please give me wisdom, Lord."

The Lord was happy. "Since you have asked for wisdom," God told me, "and not for a long life or riches for yourself or revenge on your enemies, I will give you this: I will make you wiser than anyone has ever been before now and wiser than anyone will ever be."

Wow, I thought. *That's great!* But God wasn't finished. "More than that, I will also give you what you haven't asked: I will give you riches beyond compare and honor, and a long life."

God did everything that He said. I was known for my wisdom and riches.

Who? Me?

Imagine finding a magic lamp. You rub it, and out pops a genie. What do you ask for? Be careful. Make sure your desires please God. If they don't, ask Him to change your desires.

BIBLE VERSE

"But seek first the kingdom of God and His righteousness, and all these things shall be added to you."

—*Matthew 6:33*

Hard hats, please

Solomon's temple took about 180,000 workers seven years to build. It is estimated that it would cost about 56 billion dollars to build today.

Did You Know?

The Queen of Sheba traveled to meet Solomon to test his knowledge. She wanted to see for herself if all she'd heard of his wisdom and wealth was true.

Read 1 Kings 10:1–10.

Challenge

Learn more about Solomon's wisdom.

Read 1 Kings 4:29–34.

Double Trouble

1 Kings 3:16–28

Hey, it's me, Solomon, again.

Remember what I asked God for? That's right—wisdom. Well, good thing God answered that prayer, because I was faced with a situation where I really, really needed it. Two mothers were arguing, and no one could figure out which one was telling the truth and which one was lying.

"It's my baby!" the first mother cried. "Her baby died in the middle of the night, and she switched our babies while I was asleep."

"She's a liar, King!" the other burst in. "The baby is mine! I didn't switch babies—she did! She's trying to steal my son!"

God's wisdom stirred up inside me. "Bring me a sword!" I commanded. "Cut the baby in half. Give one half to this woman, and the other half to that one."

Then the first mother cried out, "No, my king! Let the baby live, and give him to her." The other woman argued, "No, cut the baby in half!"

I knew then who was the baby's true mother. I said, "Give the baby to the first woman. She is the true mother."

Who? Me?

Wisdom is a gift God is eager to give, but you must go after it. You must search for it as if for hidden treasure. If you do, God will reward your efforts. Go for it!

A wise guy's advice

Solomon wrote the book of Proverbs. Proverbs is a collection of wise sayings and teachings about right behavior and conduct.

Did You Know?

The name Solomon means *peace* and *peaceful*. Solomon's original name was Jedidiah, which means *friend of God*. Does this make him the first Jedi?

Challenge

According to Proverbs 9:10, what is the "beginning of wisdom"?

Raven Cravings

I Kings 17:1–16

Hi, I'm Elijah.

I was a prophet. This means that God told me things He wanted me to tell others. This time, God wanted me to tell some very bad news to a very bad king named Ahab.

"God says there will not be any rain or dew for the next few years, because you lead the people away from Him," I told the king.

Then, God told me to hide by the Brook Cherith. "Drink water from the brook," God said. "I've commanded the ravens to bring you meat and bread." Then God told me to go to Zarephath. "I've commanded a widow there to feed you."

I found the widow gathering sticks for a fire. "I only have a handful of flour and a little oil," she said. "Just enough for one last cake of bread for my son and me."

"Make a cake for me first," I told her. "God will not let you run out of flour until it rains again."

The widow had great faith. She fed me, and God took care of her and her son. God never let her run out of flour or oil.

God also kept His promise to King Ahab. God did not let it rain for three years.

52

Who? Me?

Have you ever felt like giving up? The widow learned that this low time was the best time to believe in the incredible. Conquer discouragement with bodacious, action-packed belief.

BIBLE VERSE

I can do all things through Christ who strengthens me.

—Philippians 4:13

A bad guy's life story

King Ahab, the Bible tells us, did more evil in the eyes of the Lord than any other king before him.

Did You Know?

The raven is the largest member of the crow family. Ravens average 24 inches tall and have a wingspan of 46–56 inches.

Challenge

What happened to the widow's son after the drought?

Read 1 Kings 17:17–24.

God vs. Fake Gods

I Kings 18:1–39

Hi, I'm Elijah! I have a question for you. What can an imaginary god do that the One true God can't do? Absolutely nothing.

"Have all your false prophets meet me on Mount Carmel," I told King Ahab.

We killed two bulls and put the meat on two piles of wood. I challenged them. "Have your god Baal light the wood to show he is really a god."

The false prophets shouted to Baal from sunup to sundown, but of course, no fire was sent.

"Shout louder!" I teased them. "Maybe Baal's asleep! Maybe he's on vacation!" Still nothing happened.

"Drench my woodpile with water," I told them. "Do it again," I said. And just for good measure, I had them drench it again. "Show them Your power, Lord," I called up to heaven. Immediately, fire shot down from heaven. It burned up the water, the wood, and the meat on my pile. Then God's fire even burned up the stones and soil around it.

They were convinced. "The Lord—He is God!" they shouted and bowed.

54

Who? Me?

Elijah had confidence in God. He knew God would show up when he needed Him. You can have confidence that God will show up for you, too.

BIBLE VERSE

For God has not given us a spirit of fear, but of power and of love and of a sound mind.
—2 Timothy 1:7

Wanted: Elijah

Elijah was being hunted down like a criminal. King Ahab had sent soldiers into every nation and kingdom to try to capture him.

Did You Know?

Obadiah took 100 prophets and hid them 50 to a cave, feeding them only bread and water.

Read 1 Kings 18:4–5.

Challenge

How many false prophets did King Ahab have?

Read 1 Kings 18:19.

Chariot of Fire

2 Kings 2:1–18

Hi, it's me, Elijah.

I was going to heaven today. How did I know? Well, the Lord told me.

My friend and student Elisha stayed with me all day. "The Lord has called me to Bethel," I told him. "Stay here." But Elisha wouldn't hear of it. "I'm sticking with you."

God's prophets in Bethel ran to us. "God is taking your master today," they said. "I know," Elisha answered.

Then we went to Jericho. Again, God's prophets in Jericho ran up to us and told Elisha, "The Lord is taking your master from you today." "Yes," Elisha answered, "I know."

We went to the Jordan River. I rolled up my coat and slapped the water with it. Immediately, the river opened, and we crossed over on dry ground.

"What can I do for you before I go, Elisha?"

"I want a double portion of your spirit to be upon me," Elisha answered. I told him, "If you see me taken up, it shall be yours."

Suddenly, a chariot of fire and horses rushed between us, and I went up in a whirlwind as Elisha watched.

Who? Me?

Elisha wanted to learn as much as he could from Elijah. He wanted to know what Elijah knew about God. Be a good student, always eager to learn from good teachers.

BIBLE VERSE

Teach me good judgment and knowledge, for I believe Your commandments.
—Psalm 119:66

The ultimate Bible footrace?

Did Elijah outrun a horse and chariot? Sure sounds like it.

Read 1 Kings 18:44–46.

Did You Know?

Elijah and Elisha walked more than 25 miles the day Elijah was taken up into heaven.

Challenge

What did the company of prophets from Jericho want to do and what came of it?

Read 2 Kings 2:15–18.

Little Is Much

2 Kings 4:1–7

Hi, I'm Elisha.

I was a prophet of God. I wasn't the only prophet of God. There were also others who lived at the same time I did—most of whom you've never heard of. One such prophet is the focus of this story. Well, actually, his widow is.

She came to me upset. "My husband served God with all of his heart," she told me. "Now his creditor is coming to take my boys as his slaves."

"What do you have in your house?" I asked.

"Only a tiny bit of oil," she answered.

"Go ask your neighbors for empty jars," I told her. "Then go in your house and shut the door. Take your tiny bit of oil and fill up all the jars with it." So she did.

That tiny bit of oil filled up every jar she'd collected.

"Sell the oil," I told her, "and pay off your debts. Then you and your sons can live off the rest of the money."

Who? Me?

God often takes the little we can give, think up, or do and turns it into more than we could've dreamed. Do the best you can for God, and watch Him multiply it.

BIBLE VERSE

"If you have faith as a mustard seed, you will say to this mountain, 'Move from here to there,' and it will move; and nothing will be impossible for you."

— *Matthew 17:20*

Olive oil

Olive oil was highly valued in old Israel. It had lots of uses. It was used for anointings, for offerings to God, for healing purposes, for cooking, and for fueling lamps for light.

Did You Know?

Oil was used as a symbol to help people think about God's Spirit at work, too.

Challenge

What was Elisha doing when Elijah first met him?

Read 1 Kings 19:19.

The Boy Who Became King

2 Kings 22

Hi, I'm Josiah.

Do you know what I was doing when I was 8 years old? Ruling over Jerusalem as the king. I always tried to do what I thought God would want me to do.

One day I sent Shaphan, my secretary, to check on something at the temple. "Look!" Hilkiah, the high priest, said. "I have found the Book of the Law." Shaphan brought it to me. "Read it to me," I told him. After he finished, I tore my robes. "We have not obeyed the Lord very well!" I said.

Then the prophetess Huldah got a message from God. "The Lord is going to bring disaster on this place and its people because they have not obeyed the Lord. But you, King Josiah," she added, "will not see the disaster. God is going to spare you of this because your heart was tender and humble before God."

I read the whole book to everyone in my kingdom. "Destroy all the evil things and places!" I commanded. "We will obey God from now on," I told them. And the people agreed.

Who? Me?

Josiah wanted to please God but didn't completely know how. Once he heard God's word, he understood better. Read God's Word. Then follow it.

BIBLE VERSE

But he who looks into the perfect law of liberty and continues *in it,* and is not a forgetful hearer but a doer of the work, this one will be blessed in what he does.
—*James 1:25*

Passover no longer passed over

Josiah also commanded that Passover be celebrated again. This had not happened for many, many years.

Read the Passover story in Exodus 12.

Did You Know?

Josiah was king for 31 years. He was killed in a battle. His son Jehoahaz became king after him.

Challenge

How is King Josiah described at the end of his life?

Read 2 Kings 23:25.

61

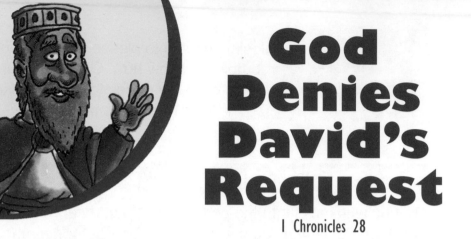

God Denies David's Request

I Chronicles 28

Hi there. Remember me? I'm David.

I killed the giant Goliath. I brought the ark of God back to Jerusalem. I wrote songs to God. Here's what I am happiest about: God called me "a man after His own heart."

I wanted so much to please God. I wanted to do something special for Him. So I decided I'd build God a house—a temple. I wanted it to be the most amazing building ever built. But God wouldn't let me build it. "Your son Solomon will build it for Me," God said.

"Solomon," I said, "serve God with all of your heart all the days of your life. If you will seek Him, you will find Him. If you forsake Him, He will reject you." I gave Solomon the plans for the temple. "Be strong and do this work that God has called you to do."

Who? Me?

David gives his son, Solomon, a task. However, David knows he will not be around to make sure Solomon does it. Can your parents count on you to do the tasks they give you?

BIBLE VERSE

And whatever you do, do it heartily, as to the Lord and not to men, knowing that from the Lord you will receive the reward of the inheritance; for you serve the Lord Christ.
—*Colossians 3:23–24*

A good life remembered . . .

David was king for 40 years. He died at a good old age (probably around age 70), having enjoyed long life, wealth, and honor.

Did You Know?

David had many sons. Of all his sons, the Bible says, God *chose* Solomon to become king after David's death.

Challenge

Why did God not allow David to build the temple?

Read
1 Chronicles 28:3.

A House for God

2 Chronicles 2–3

Hey again! It's me, Solomon. Did you know I built a house for God? Talk about big jobs!

"This must be a glorious place," I said. "It is *God's* house." I often worried that the job was too much for any man—especially me. "Who am I to build a temple for God?" I asked.

I hired the best artists, craftsmen, and workers. I used the best materials. I sought help from some of the world's most powerful people. Hiram, the king of Tyre, gave us beautiful cedar, pine, and juniper logs from Lebanon.

"Send me a man skilled to work in gold and bronze," I asked King Hiram. "Artists gifted with purple, red, and blue yarn; experienced engravers; men who are skilled in cutting wood." And King Hiram did.

We covered the ceiling beams, doorframes, walls, and doors with gold. Seven years later—thanks to the hard work of thousands and thousands of workers—the temple was finally finished.

Who? Me?

Solomon could've been lazy or careless with this task. Instead, he pushed himself to excel. Always demand the very best from yourself in every job you do.

Hiram's Huram . . .

King Hiram sent Huram, a skilled craftsman, to help Solomon. Huram made many things, including 30 gold basins, 1,000 silver basins, 30 golden bowls, 40 silver bowls, and over a thousand other vessels. He also covered the altar in gold and manufactured gold flowers, lamps, snuffers, tongs, cups, incense dishes, pans to hold burning charcoal, and hinges for the inner and outer doors.

Did You Know?

The wood King Hiram provided most likely came from around the small town of Barouk. To this day, the forests of Barouk contain more than two million cedar trees.

Challenge

How did they get the big logs from Lebanon to Jerusalem?

Read 2 Chronicles 2:16.

A New Temple

Ezra 1

Hi, I'm Cyrus, king of Persia.

Although I am not a Jew or Hebrew, I helped the Jews rebuild their temple.

What's that? You didn't know their temple needed to be rebuilt? Let me fill in some history for you. King Solomon had built a beautiful temple for God. It stood for 374 years. Then Nebuchadnezzar, king of Babylon, totally destroyed it and took the Jews captive.

This was where I came in. I conquered Babylon. I can't explain it, but I had the strongest sense that God was telling me to help the Jews get back to their homeland so they could rebuild that glorious temple.

"God has appointed me," I announced to all, "to build a temple for Him at Jerusalem in Judah." I urged the Jews in my kingdom to go back to Jerusalem to do the work. I also gave them all the things King Nebuchadnezzar had stolen from the temple.

More than 42,000 Jews left in a paradelike celebration to do this great work.

Who? Me?

It's easy to do a task cheerfully when you're treated—as King Cyrus treated the Jews—with kindness. How do you act when the one in charge is unkind or angry? Determine to be a blessing even when life treats you unkindly.

BIBLE VERSE

Servants, *be* submissive to *your* masters with all fear, not only to the good and gentle, but also to the harsh. For this *is* commendable, if because of conscience toward God one endures grief, suffering wrongfully.
—*1 Peter 2:18–19*

A Bible mystery . . .

Isaiah prophesied that Cyrus would do this for the Jews. Amazingly, Isaiah said this—calling Cyrus by his name—over 150 years before Cyrus was even born! Did Cyrus discover Isaiah's prophecy?

Did You Know?

This second temple lasted 584 years. It was destroyed by fire in AD 70.

Challenge

Did God actually live in the temple?

Read Acts 7:47–50.

Rebuilding My Hometown

Nehemiah 1–4

Hi, I'm Nehemiah.

I worked as a cupbearer for King Artaxerxes. I would taste the drinks first to make sure no one was trying to kill the king by putting poison in his drink. I had a dangerous job.

One day I asked my friends about my hometown. "How are things in Jerusalem?" Their answer broke my heart. "The town is in ruins," they said. "The walls around Jerusalem are broken, and the people are upset." I cried and cried and didn't eat for days. "God," I prayed, "we have sinned. Please forgive us and bring us back together as a people."

"What's wrong, Nehemiah?" King Artaxerxes asked. "My homeland is in ruins," I said. King Artaxerxes helped me return to Jerusalem so I could rebuild the walls.

We made great progress on the walls. Many fellow Jews helped, but not everyone was happy about the effort. We were attacked many times by those who wanted to stop us, but God protected us. We had to rebuild and fight at the same time. We kept our tool in one hand and our sword or spear in the other.

Who? Me?

Do the good you know you should do, but don't be surprised if you find some people unhappy about it. Press on like Nehemiah did. Don't stop because someone criticizes you, makes fun of you, or disagrees with you. Be bold.

BIBLE VERSE

And not only *that*, but we also glory in tribulations, knowing that tribulation produces perseverance; and perseverance, character; and character, hope.

—*Romans 5:3–4*

Do something—fast!

Nehemiah fasted. To fast means *to stop eating* for a short period of time. Fasting helps you think more seriously about spiritual things and less about unimportant things.

Did You Know?

Nehemiah said a quick prayer before answering King Artaxerxes' question about why he was sad. God is always listening. Prayers do not need to be long or formal—just sincere.

Challenge

Nehemiah was very generous. How many ate with him each day?

Read Nehemiah 5:17.

Hooray for the Queen!

Esther 2–7

Hello, I'm Mordecai.

You're probably more familiar with my famous, beautiful, and much younger cousin, Esther—whom I raised as my own child after her parents died.

Esther, you may know, became a queen. King Ahasuerus held a huge contest to find a wife. This was not just a one-day event, mind you. No, no, no. Each girl received beauty treatments for a full year before she even met the king. Esther won the hearts of everyone in the palace—including the king's heart.

I, on the other hand, ran into unwanted trouble with one of the king's commanders. "Bow to me!" Haman ordered. But I wouldn't bow to any man—only to God. Next thing I know, Haman is out to kill me—and every Jew.

"Esther," I said, "you must tell the king." Esther bravely agreed. "I will go to the king even if it costs me my life." The king listened to Esther. "Who is trying to kill your people?" he asked. "Haman," she told him.

King Ahasuerus punished Haman severely, then gave his job to me. Esther's courage had saved the Jewish people.

70

Who? Me?

Esther risked her life to get an audience with King Ahasuerus. Oftentimes it takes courage to do the right thing. Don't turn away when you see unfairness. Have courage. God is with you.

Pride goes before a 75-foot fall . . .

Haman's hatred for Mordecai led him to his own death. Haman built a 75-foot-tall gallows on which to hang Mordecai, but ended up being hanged on it himself.

Did You Know?

Esther was originally named *Hadassah*. Later she was called *Esther*, which is from the Persian word *satarah* and means *a star*.

Challenge

Why did Haman have to create a miniparade in Mordecai's honor?

Read Esther 6:1–12.

Never Give Up

Job 1–2

Hi, I'm Job.

Maybe you've heard an older adult say something about "the patience of Job." Are you wondering, *Why would anyone say that?* I'll tell you exactly why.

I had a great life. I had a big family, servants, plenty of food, and good health. I *had* these things. I also had these things taken away from me—in a single day!

"Job!" someone ran to me, shouting. "All your donkeys and oxen have been stolen! And bad guys have killed your servants!" Before I could catch my breath, someone else said, "Fire fell from heaven and killed all your sheep and shepherds!" Another person added, "All your camels and workers are dead!" Then, to my deeper horror, "A house caved in and killed all your sons and daughters!"

I fell to the ground in shock, but I didn't get mad at God. "This is very bad, but God is still good," I said.

Soon I got sores all over my body. "Curse God and end this suffering," my wife shouted at me. "No," I said patiently. "Good or bad, I will praise God."

In time, I did lose my patience, but God was kind to me and gave me a good life again.

72

Who? Me?

It's easy to praise God when good things happen. The challenge is to still praise God when things are bad. In good times and bad, God is still there, still cares, and is still good.

BIBLE VERSE

Though the fig tree may not blossom, nor fruit be on the vines; though the labor of the olive may fail, and the fields yield no food; though the flock may be cut off from the fold, and there be no herd in the stalls—yet I will rejoice in the LORD, I will joy in the God of my salvation.
—Habakkuk 3:17–18

A fire-breathing dragon?

Is God describing a fire-breathing dragon when He is talking to Job? (Read Job 41:12–34.) Many say no. Some say God is talking about a crocodile. What do you think?

Did You Know?

God makes the waves stop. God keeps storehouses of snow. God gives the morning orders. God knows when the mountain goats have babies.

Read Job 38–39.

Challenge

How many years after all this trouble did Job live?

Read Job 42:16.

73

A Truth-Sayer

Jeremiah 36

Hi there. My name is Jeremiah. I was a prophet of God.

God would tell me things He wanted me to tell others. It was my job to tell them whether the word of the Lord was pleasant or unpleasant.

"Take a scroll," God told me, "and write down all the things I've been telling you about Israel, Judah, and the other nations. Maybe the people will turn back to Me when they hear about the disaster their sins are bringing upon them. Maybe they'll stop being wicked. If so, I'll forgive them."

I called my scribe to write as I spoke God's words to him. "I can't go to the temple, Baruch," I explained. "So you go. Read these words to the people for me." Baruch did what I asked. "Read it to us also," the temple officials said. So Baruch read it to them. They were terrified at what they heard. "We must read this to the king," they said.

However, when King Jehoiakim heard the words, he ignored them and threw the scroll into the fire. He didn't feel scared, sorry, or interested in what God had said.

Who? Me?

King Jehoiakim was punished for his hardheartedness. God wants us to listen to Him, to respect Him, and to humbly obey His word. Be tender-hearted toward God.

The weeping prophet

Jeremiah is often called the weeping prophet because he cried often and deeply over the sins of Israel, and because he saw the punishments that were coming against Israel because of their hardheartedness toward God.

Did You Know?

All of Jeremiah's warnings were ignored. He was laughed at, locked in a dungeon, and thrown into a deep muddy pit where he almost died.

Challenge

Why did Baruch and Jeremiah have to hide?

Read Jeremiah 36:26.

The Living Bones

Ezekiel 37:1–14

Hi there. I'm Ezekiel, a prophet of God.

God often spoke to me through visions. He'd create a dream to teach me and then, mysteriously, place me inside that dream. It was quite dramatic and memorable.

One such dream was especially vivid. In it, God took me to a valley. The valley was full of bones. Old bones. Brittle bones. Bones that would snap in two if I picked them up. "Son of man," God said to me, "can these bones live?"

"Only You know, Lord," I answered. "Tell them to live," God said. "Live, bones," I said. Suddenly, there was a loud clatter, like sticks banging. I looked and the bones were connecting themselves together. Then tendon and new flesh appeared over them. "Tell them to breathe," God told me. So I did.

"These bones are My people," God explained. "They have lost all hope. But I have not forgotten them. I will bring them back together again, and they will know that I am the Lord their God."

Who? Me?

God's people had forgotten Him. But God had not forgotten them. When sin makes you turn away from God, turn back. Tell God you're sorry. If you are truly sorry, He will always forgive you.

BIBLE VERSE

If we confess our sins, He is faithful and just to forgive us *our* sins and to cleanse us from all unrighteousness.

—1 John 1:9

Lights! Camera! Action!

Ezekiel expressed God's messages in very dramatic ways. Once he was told to shake when he ate his food and to shudder fearfully when he drank water. In these ways, he showed what life would be like because of the violence of the people.

Challenge

Why did Ezekiel have to lie on his left side for 390 days?

Read Ezekiel 4:4–5.

Did You Know?

God once had Ezekiel shave his head and beard and then burn the hair.

Read Ezekiel 5:1–2.

Can You Stand the Heat?

Daniel 3

Hi, I'm Shadrach. I'm Meshach. And I'm Abednego.*

You might have heard about our experience in King Nebuchadnezzar's fiery furnace. "Bow down and worship me," the king demanded, "or be burned." The music began and everyone bowed down—everyone, that is, except us.

We went into the fiery furnace as three—but once inside, we were four. God met us in the fire. King Nebuchadnezzar was amazed, called us out, discovered that we didn't even smell like smoke, and immediately became a follower of God, too.

Dramatic stuff, right? Faith is dramatic! Faith stands when everyone around bows. Faith says, "I will obey God no matter what."

*Sometimes Abednego's name is spelled Abed-Nego.

78

Who? Me?

Will you say "No!" when your best friends say "Yes!"—but you know they are wrong? Shadrach, Meshach, and Abednego's dramatic faith changed the life of a king and his country. Your dramatic faith can change the world, too.

BIBLE VERSE

"If that *is the case*, our God whom we serve is able to deliver us from the burning fiery furnace, and He will deliver us from your hand, O king. But if not, let it be known to you, O king, that we do not serve your gods, nor will we worship the gold image which you have set up."
—Daniel 3:17–18

God works in mysterious ways . . .

Which powerful ruler ate grass like a cow, lived outdoors like an animal, grew hair all over his body as thick as an eagle's feathers, and had nails like the claws of a bird?

Find out by reading Daniel 4.

Did You Know?

Shadrach, Meshach, and Abednego were buddies with Daniel.

Read Daniel 1.

Challenge

What did Nebuchadnezzar say when he saw their dramatic faith?

Read Daniel 3:28–29.

The Lions Sleep Tonight . . .

Daniel 6

Hello. My name is Daniel.

King Darius was going to put me in charge of his whole kingdom. My coworkers didn't like that idea, so they tried to get me in trouble.

"Daniel prays all the time," someone said. "Let's trick King Darius into making it a crime to pray to anyone or anything but King Darius." So they did. "New law!" they announced. "Pray only to King Darius or die in the den of lions!"

King Darius knew he'd been tricked. "I hope your God rescues you from these lions, Daniel," he said. He worried about me all night long. There was no need for worry, though, because God sent an angel who protected me from the lions.

"Daniel," the king called. "Has your God saved you?" "Yes, King Darius!" I answered as they lifted me out. King Darius was so pleased. "Throw these false accusers into the den," the king commanded. "From now on, we will serve the God Daniel serves!"

Who? Me?

Obeying God is more important than any man-made rule or law. Keep God's commands at the very top of your list of priorities.

BIBLE VERSE

"But seek first the kingdom of God and His righteousness, and all these things shall be added to you."

—Matthew 6:33

Your sins will find you out . . .

As is so often the case, the bad guys' plan blew up in their faces. Not only did *they* pay for their folly, but their wives and children became victims of their deception, too.

Read Daniel 6:24.

Did You Know?

Daniel lived most of his long life in and around the king's palace.

Challenge

How many times a day did Daniel pray?

Read Daniel 6:10.

Splish, Splash, Get Back on the Right Path . . .

Jonah 1–4

Hi, I'm Jonah.

You probably already know my story. It's one of the most famous stories in the world.

"Go to Nineveh," God told me. "Tell them to stop doing evil." But I tried to run away from God. I got on a boat and headed off. Then, you guessed it, a storm came and nearly sank the ship. "It's my fault," I finally confessed. "I'm running from God. Throw me overboard." They did. I sank. Then—*GULP!*

After a few days in the gut of a fish, thinking and praying, I said, "I'll go to Nineveh, Lord." Then—*BLOOTCH!* I was burped onto dry land.

I preached in the streets of Nineveh for 40 days. Then, to my dismay, the people of Nineveh turned from their sins and cried out to God. "I knew this would happen," I fussed at God. "I knew You'd forgive these wicked people because You are a loving and gracious God."

"Why should you be angry about this, Jonah?" God asked me. "I love all people."

82

Who? Me?

Loving people you like is easy. But how do you treat the ones you can't stand being around? God loves every person. You should love them, too.

BIBLE VERSE

"But love your enemies, do good, and lend, hoping for nothing in return; and your reward will be great, and you will be sons of the Most High. For He is kind to the unthankful and evil."

—*Luke 6:35*

What was Nineveh like?

Nineveh, the Bible tells us, was a very impressive city. It wasn't a tiny town by any means. God Himself told Jonah that Nineveh had more than 120,000 people in it. Read Jonah 4:11.

Did You Know?

Nineveh was located on the Tigris River across from modern-day Mosul, Iraq.

Challenge

How many days and nights was Jonah inside the big fish?

Read Jonah 1:17.

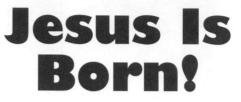

Jesus Is Born!

Matthew 1:18–2:12
Luke 1:26–2:20

Hi, I'm Mary. God sent an angel to tell me something amazing.

"Greetings!" the angel Gabriel began. "The Lord is with you." I was afraid. *Why would God send an angel to me?*

"You're going to have a baby," Gabriel told me. "Name Him Jesus. He will be a great king. His kingdom will never end."

Gabriel told me that my cousin Elizabeth—who was very old—was going to have a baby, too. I'm sure I looked surprised. "Nothing is impossible with God," Gabriel told me. "I am God's servant," I told Gabriel. "May all that you've said happen."

Joseph and I went to Bethlehem. I gave birth to a baby boy there. I stared in amazement at Him for so long. "Hello, baby Jesus," I said.

Shepherds came telling us about angels appearing in the sky. "A Savior has been born in Bethlehem," they told us. Then they sang happily to God.

These were marvelous things. I pondered them often.

Who? Me?

God's plan changed Mary's life forever. And while it was a wonderful gift to Mary, it also brought Mary challenges she would not have faced had she told God "No." Are you willing to do anything for God? If you are, God will certainly use you for good.

BIBLE VERSE

I delight to do Your will, O my God, and Your law *is* within my heart.

—*Psalm 40:8*

Christmas legend

The Bible never says there were three wise men. Many think of it as three because three gifts were given. The Bible says that "wise men from the East came." It does not tell us how many.

Read Matthew 2.

Did You Know?

The Gospels of Mark and John do not include any details about the birth of Jesus. We learn about Jesus' birth in the Gospels of Matthew and Luke.

Challenge

What gifts did the wise men give to Jesus?

Read Matthew 2:11

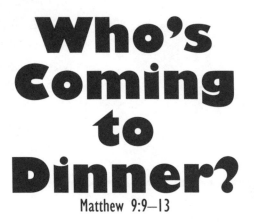

Who's Coming to Dinner?

Matthew 9:9–13

Hi, I'm Matthew.

Jesus chose me to be one of His 12 disciples. I saw Him heal many people. I saw Him walk on water. I ate with Him often. Jesus was my friend. Indeed, Jesus wanted to be my friend when almost no one else did.

You see, I was a tax collector. Whenever people saw me, they'd avoid me. "All he wants is my money," they'd say. And they'd be right. Collecting money was my job. Sometimes, I collected more than people really owed. No wonder I did not have many friends.

But Jesus was my friend. "Follow me," He said. And I did. He ate at my house with me and other tax collectors I knew. "Why does Jesus eat with collectors and sinners?" asked with a sneer.

althy don't need a doctor," Jesus answered them. "Sick hen Jesus added, "God wants to see mercy more than think they liked that, either.

Who? Me?

Matthew knew he needed God's forgiveness and mercy. The Pharisees thought of themselves as too good to need it. Admit your sins to God and thank Him for His forgiveness.

> ### BIBLE VERSE
>
> If we confess our sins, He is faithful and just to forgive us *our* sins and to cleanse us from all unrighteousness.
>
> —*1 John 1:9*

God helps the outcasts . . .

Matthew was a publican, which means *tax collector.* He collected a Roman tax called a *custom* or *toll.* He'd set up at the city gates, along well-traveled roads, or near the busy temple. Publicans were often considered as among the lowest of society.

Did You Know?
The Gospels of Mark and Luke called Matthew by the name of *Levi.*

Challenge
How does Hosea 6:6 relate to this story?

How to Feed 5,000 People

Matthew 14:13–21; Mark 6:30–44
Luke 9:10–17; John 6:1–14

Hi, I'm Peter.

I was one of Jesus' closest friends. He was my Lord and Teacher. I loved spending time with Jesus. Every day was so amazing. It seemed everywhere Jesus went a crowd would follow.

One time we were way out in the countryside, a long walk from the nearest town. It was getting late in the day. "Master," we said to Jesus, "send the crowds away so they can get to the villages in time to buy something to eat." Jesus looked at us, then said, "You feed them." *Feed all these people?* We were confused. "But, Master," we explained, "there are over five thousand people here! This boy only has five loaves of bread and two small fish."

"Have everyone sit down," Jesus told us. So we did. Jesus took the five loaves of bread and two fish, looked up to heaven, said a prayer, then had us pass out the food to everyone.

Amazingly, everyone had plenty to eat. We never ran out of bread or fish! In fact, we had leftovers!

Who? Me?

Jesus took care of people's needs. He helped people when they needed help. God wants us to do the same. Be a helper to those around you today.

BIBLE VERSE

But whoever has this world's goods, and sees his brother in need, and shuts up his heart from him, how does the love of God abide in him?

—*1 John 3:17*

You do the math . . .

Actually, the number of people fed was probably closer to twice this number. The Bible says there were 5,000 *men*. Many would've had their wives with them as well as their children.

Challenge

How much food was left over?

Read Luke 9:17.

Did You Know?

The Gospel of John tells us it was a boy who shared his meal first.

Read John 6:9.

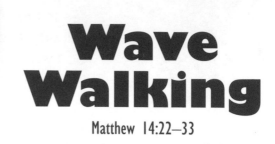

Wave Walking

Matthew 14:22–33

Hello again, it's me, Peter.

I wanted to tell you what happened after we fed those 5,000 people and collected the leftovers. Jesus told us to get in the boat. "I'll meet you later on the other side," He told us. So we got in the boat.

Late in the night, we looked up and saw Someone walking on water! "It's a ghost!" we cried out. Then we heard Jesus' calming voice. "Don't be afraid," He told us. "It's Me." *How amazing is this?* I thought. "If it really is You, Lord," I yelled out, "tell me to come out there on the water with You." Jesus said, "Come on out."

I stepped out of the boat onto the water. I was actually walking on the water! Then I looked at the big waves and this thought hit me: *Am I crazy? I can't walk on water!*

Immediately, I began to sink. "Help me, Lord!" I cried. Jesus caught me. He looked both a little surprised and a little disappointed. He asked me, "Why did you doubt?"

Who? Me?

A tiny bit of fear can go a long, long way. Fear locks you in an invisible prison. Faith in God is the key that unlocks it. Don't let fear control you.

BIBLE VERSE

Whenever I am afraid, I will trust in You.

—*Psalm 56:3*

Let's go boating . . .

In 1986, an ancient fishing boat was discovered in the Sea of Galilee. It was just like the boat the disciples might've used. It was 26.5 feet long, 7.5 feet wide, and 4.5 feet deep. It could carry more than one ton of weight and had room for 15 passengers. The boat is now housed in Kibbutz Ginossar in Israel, and it is sometimes called the Galilee Boat. You can find out more about this remarkable boat on the Internet or through your local library.

Did You Know?

The Sea of Galilee Jesus walked on is also known as the Lake of Gennesaret and Lake Tiberias. It is 7.5 miles wide and 12.5 miles long today.

Challenge

What did Jesus do after He sent His disciples away?

Read Matthew 14:22–23.

Liar, Liar

Matthew 26:31–35, 69–75
Mark 14:66–72; Luke 22:54–62

Hey, it's me, Peter.

I want to tell you about one of the saddest days of my life. And—here's the truth of it—I brought it on myself.

We had just eaten a special Passover meal together when Jesus told us we'd each run away from Him that night. "Not me!" I insisted. "I never will!" Jesus looked at me. "Three times before the rooster crows again, Peter, you will say you don't even know Me." "No, Lord," I promised, "I will never do that." But when the crowd came to arrest Jesus, I ran away.

I sneakily followed the angry crowd into town. A girl walked up to me and announced, "He was with Jesus!" "No!" I said. "I don't know what you're talking about." Then it happened again. "This man was with Jesus," another girl said. I told her, "I don't know the Man."

A bit later others said, "You're one of Jesus' men!" I shouted back, "I'm telling you, I've never even met Jesus!" Immediately, I heard a rooster crow. Jesus had been right. I ran away and cried and cried.

Who? Me?

Are you proud to know Jesus? Are you proud that He's your Savior and friend? Speak out boldly for Jesus. Let others know that you love Him.

BIBLE VERSE

"Therefore whoever confesses Me before men, him I will also confess before My Father who is in heaven."

—Matthew 10:32

Peter is forgiven . . .

After Jesus came back to life, He assured Peter that He still loved him. "Do you love Me?" Jesus asked Peter. "You know I love You, Lord," Peter answered. Jesus asked Peter this three times—once for each time he denied Him. Then Jesus gave Peter this charge: "Feed My sheep," He said. And Peter spent the rest of his life doing just that.

Did You Know?

Peter was originally named Simon. Jesus gave him the name Cephas, which in Aramaic means *rock*. Cephas in Greek is translated as *Petra*, which in English is Peter.

Challenge

What was Jesus doing right before He was arrested?

Read Matthew 26:44–48.

93

Walking Tall

Mark 2:1–12; Matthew 9:1–8;
Luke 5:17–26

Hi, I am someone whose life was completely changed by the healing power of Jesus and by the kindness of four great friends.

You might have read about me. My legs didn't work at all, so my friends picked me up on my mat and carried me to a house where Jesus was preaching. It was so crowded, we couldn't get in. My friends came up with a very unusual idea.

They took me up on top of the house, made a hole through the the roof, and lowered me down in front of Jesus. Jesus told me, "Son, your sins are forgiven." I liked hearing that, but it made some folks mad. *Does Jesus think He's God?* they thought to themselves.

Jesus looked right at them. "Is it easier to say, 'Your sins are forgiven,'" He asked them, "or to tell this paralyzed man to get up and walk?" The men didn't answer. Jesus told me, "Get up, take up your bed, and walk home." My legs were healed that very moment. I got up, grabbed my mat, and walked home.

94

Who? Me?

This guy had some great friends. God wants us to be great friends to others, too—especially to those who need help. Help the needy as much as you can. This pleases God.

BIBLE VERSE

"Give, and it will be given to you: good measure, pressed down, shaken together, and running over will be put into your bosom. For with the same measure that you use, it will be measured back to you."

—Luke 6:38

Whose house was it?

The Bible doesn't tell us whose house Jesus was preaching in. Was it Peter's house? Or was it someone else's house? We do know that in Mark 1:29 we are told Peter had a house in Capernaum.

Did You Know?

Capernaum was a small, poor fishing village during Jesus' lifetime, with only 1,000 to 1,500 people living there at the time.

Challenge

Who got upset when Jesus said, "Son, your sins are forgiven"?

Read Mark 2:6–7.

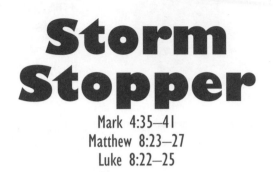

Storm Stopper

Mark 4:35–41
Matthew 8:23–27
Luke 8:22–25

Hey, it's me, Peter.

I've got to tell you this amazing story about Jesus.

One evening all of us were in a boat going across the Sea of Galilee. It was a beautiful time of the day to be on the water. Very relaxing. Jesus was tired after preaching all day to a huge crowd. He found a cushion in the back of the boat and fell sound asleep. Then—out of nowhere—a huge storm appeared. Suddenly, we were struggling to keep the boat from sinking.

"We're going to drown!" we cried. Then we yelled as loud as we could, "Wake up, Jesus! Help us!"

Jesus woke up, stood up, and started talking right to the waves. "Be still!" He told them.

"Hush!" Immediately, the sea became as smooth as glass. I mean, not a ripple. It was so amazing, it scared us. "What kind of man is this?" we asked each other. "Even the winds and the waves obey Him!"

Who? Me?

We all get scared sometimes—just like the apostles did. But we don't have to stay afraid. Instead, we can pray. Tell God when you're feeling scared. Then take a slow, deep breath and relax.

BIBLE VERSE

But you must continue in the things which you have learned and been assured of, knowing from whom you have learned *them*.

—*2 Timothy 3:14*

Severe weather warning

The Bible says this was a "great tempest" (which means a bad storm), and that they were in "jeopardy" (which means great danger). It must've been pretty serious to scare these tough guys. Four out of the 12 apostles were skilled boatsmen.

Did You Know?

God tells each wave where to stop.

Read Job 38:11.

Challenge

Who else in the Bible slept on a boat during a bad storm?

Read Jonah 1:4–6.

A Jesus Parade!

Mark 11:1–11
Matthew 21:1–11
Luke 19:28–40

Greetings again! It's me, Peter.

I want to tell you about the time Jesus rode a donkey to Jerusalem.

Jerusalem is a very important city. It's called the City of David and it has been around for thousands of years. It is the home of the first and second temples, and all the busyness and crowds that brings.

"Go ahead of Me," Jesus said. "Bring Me the donkey you'll find tied there." We put some coats on the donkey for Jesus to sit on. There was a huge crowd cheering for Jesus as He rode in. Some people put their cloaks on the road like you would do if a king were riding in—which, in fact, was exactly what was happening. Jerusalem was being visited by the King of kings!

"Hosanna!" they shouted. "Blessed is He who comes in the name of the Lord!" they cheered. You could hear the celebration all over the city.

"Make them be quiet!" the temple teachers protested. But Jesus smiled and said, "If they get quiet, the stones will start cheering."

Who? Me?

Jesus always deserves our praise. Praising Jesus makes our faith stronger. You can praise Him with shouts, with songs, with instruments, with poems—you name it! Praise God right now.

BIBLE VERSE

Praise the LORD! Oh, give thanks to the LORD, for *He* is good! For His mercy *endures* forever.

—*Psalm 106:1*

O Jerusalem, Jerusalem . . .

Ultimately, Jerusalem rejected Jesus. Listen to what Jesus said to the people: "O Jerusalem, Jerusalem, the one who kills the prophets and stones those who are sent to her! How often I wanted to gather your children together, as a hen gathers her chicks under *her* wings, but you were not willing!" (Matthew 23:37).

Did You Know?

The ancient Hebrews made cleanliness and hygiene an important part of life. The temple courtyard, for example, held 2,000 baths where worshipers washed their hands and feet before going into the sanctuary.

Challenge

What did Jesus cry as He was about to enter Jerusalem?

Read Luke 19:41–44.

Searching for Jesus

Luke 2:39–52

Hello there. I am Joseph—Mary's husband.

I like to think of Jesus as my son, because I raised Him. But Jesus was God's Son. What a joy it was to watch Him grow up into a man.

Each year we went to Jerusalem to celebrate the Feast of the Passover. We always traveled in a large group of friends and relatives. On one of these trips—Jesus was 12 years old at this time—we had journeyed a full day back home before realizing that Jesus wasn't with our group. *Had we accidentally left Him behind?* We were worried. *Was He lost?* Was He trying to find us, too?

Mary and I hurried back to Jerusalem. "Jesus," we called. "Jesus, where are You?" We searched for Him for three days before we spotted Him. He was in the temple, surrounded by all these wise teachers. They couldn't believe how wise He was.

"We've been looking everywhere for You," Mary told Him. "Didn't you know I'd be in My Father's house?" He asked. Then we went home together.

Who? Me?

Jesus sets the perfect example for young people. You don't have to wait until you're grown to get serious about serving God. Serve Him passionately starting today.

BIBLE VERSE

Let no one despise your youth, but be an example to the believers in word, in conduct, in love, in spirit, in faith, in purity.

—*1 Timothy 4:12*

School days . . .

The Mishnah is an important ancient Jewish book. It tells us that children often began studying the books of Moses—known in the Jewish faith as the *Torah*—at age 5, studied oral traditions at age 12, and became religious adults at age 13.

Did You Know?

Jesus spent a great deal of time in synagogues.

Read Matthew 4:23.

Challenge

How did Mary feel as she thought back on this experience?

Read Luke 2:51.

A Dove from Heaven

Luke 3:1–22; Matthew 3:13–17
Mark 1:4–11; John 1:29–34

Hi! I'm John the Baptist.

I lived in the desert. My clothing was made from camel's hair, and I wore a leather belt around my waist. Guess what I ate? Locusts and wild honey. I am sometimes called John the Baptizer, because I baptized so many people.

When people from the villages came to see me, I would tell them plainly: "Repent! Change! Stop doing wrong! Start doing right!" Many wanted God's forgiveness.

I also told them God's kingdom was near. "Someone more powerful than me is coming," I warned them. "Now is the time to live right!" I said. Then one day, Jesus showed up. I said, "Look! The Lamb of God who takes away the sins of the world."

"Baptize Me," Jesus said. "But You should be baptizing me," I told Him. "It is the right thing to do," Jesus explained.

After I baptized Jesus, I saw a dove come from heaven. "This is My Son," God spoke. "I'm very pleased with Him."

102

Who? Me?

The word repent means *to feel regret about bad things you've done.* It is the first step to peace with God. Is there something you need to repent? Talk to God about it now.

Dinner is served . . .

In ancient Greece and Rome, fried locusts, cicadas, and grasshoppers were considered superior to the best meat or fish. Locusts are a good source of protein, vitamins, and minerals and are still eaten in Asia today.

Challenge

How did John answer the people when they asked: "What shall we do?"

Read Luke 3:10–14.

Did You Know?

Leviticus 11:22 says: "These you may eat: the locust after its kind, the destroying locust after its kind, the cricket after its kind, and the grasshopper after its kind."

Tempted in the Desert

Luke 4:1–13; Matthew 4:1–11
Mark 1:12–13

Hi, I'm Luke.

I was a doctor. But I think my Bible books have helped more people than I ever did in my medical practice. Here's a story from one of those books:

After Jesus was baptized, the Holy Spirit led Him to the desert to be tempted by the devil. He stayed out there for 40 days. He did not eat nor drink, so He was very weak and thirsty.

"If You're the Son of God," the devil taunted, "make these stones bread." Jesus answered, "Man does not live on bread alone." The devil led Jesus to a place so high they could see all the kingdoms of the world. "I'll give You all this," the devil hissed, "if You'll worship me." Jesus answered: "It's written: 'Worship and serve God only.'"

Next, the devil stood Jesus on the highest point of the temple. "If You're the Son of God," he snapped, "jump! The Scriptures say God will keep You from getting hurt." Jesus told him, "It also says: 'Do not put God to the test.'"

Finally, the devil left Jesus alone, and waited for another opportunity.

104

Who? Me?

It isn't a sin to be tempted—Jesus was tempted. It becomes sin when we give in to the temptation. Sin is like a sticky spider's web—it's hard to break free from it. Say "No!" to each temptation.

Dear Doctor Luke . . .

Luke used medical terms more often than other New Testament writers. For instance, when he wrote of Publius' father being sick (Acts 28:8), he added what type of sickness he had: a fever and dysentery.

Challenge

Who helped Jesus after the devil left?

Read Matthew 4:11.

Did You Know?

Luke is the only Bible book author who wasn't a Jew.

A Thankless Job

Luke 17:11–19

Hi, I am a leper. That is, I *used* to be a leper.

I had a very serious disease called *leprosy*. I had to live outside the town with other lepers, far away from healthy people and my family. Worse than that, there was no cure for this disease.

So how could I stop being a leper, if there wasn't a cure? Great question. Easy answer: Jesus!

We saw Jesus walking. "Have mercy!" we cried. And Jesus did. "Go," He said. "Show yourselves to the priests." A rush of excitement and confidence fell over us. All ten of us hurried toward the temple. And as we ran, our skin cleared up, and our leprosy was healed! We could be with our families and friends again!

I couldn't stop praising God! I was shouting and dancing and jumping around all the way back to Jesus. "Thank You, Jesus!" I cried as I fell at His feet. "Thank You!"

"Didn't I heal ten lepers?" Jesus asked me. "Where are the other nine?" I didn't know what to say. "Has only one come back to thank Me? Go," He said. "Your faith has healed you."

Who? Me?

It is so important to say "thank you." It's more than simply showing good manners—the experience is unfinished without it. Make sure the people who help you know how much you appreciate them.

BIBLE VERSE

"Oh, give thanks to the LORD, for *He is* good! For His mercy *endures* forever."

—*1 Chronicles 16:34*

Leprosy today?

Today, there is a cure and treatment for leprosy (now known as *Hansen's disease*). Even so, there were almost 700,000 cases of leprosy in 2004—over 70,000 of which were children. The good news is, there are fewer and fewer cases each year.

Did You Know?

The only one to come back and thank Jesus was a Samaritan. The others—Jesus' countrymen—didn't return.

Challenge

Where was Jesus on His way to?

Read Luke 17:11.

Jesus and Kids

Luke 18:15–17; Matthew 19:13–15
Mark 10:13–16

Hello again. It's me, Peter!

Everywhere we went, crowds of people from all around would surround us. Jesus would teach them, heal them, touch them, and hug them—for hours! Jesus was definitely a people-person! He loved each and every one of them. And I mean every one—rich and poor, tall and short, men and women, old and young.

As a matter of fact, Jesus seemed especially fond of the younger ones. "Be like children," He told us. "God loves it when children praise Him," He said. No doubt about it, Jesus loved kids.

So why did we once try to keep kids from getting closer to Jesus? I don't have a good answer for that one, but I can tell you Jesus put us straight about it—and I mean quick. "Let the children come to Me," He told us. "Don't stop them."

Who? Me?

Jesus didn't treat one kind of person one way and another kind of person another way. Jesus loved all people the same. Think of each person you meet as a treasured child of God. Then treat them likewise.

Jesus treated people better

Women and children were viewed as less important than men in Palestine in New Testament times—though Jesus clearly disagreed. While children—especially boys—were prized by parents in public, they were mostly ignored as unimportant.

Did You Know?

Jesus said you couldn't enter the kingdom of God unless you became like a child.

Read Mark 10:15.

Challenge

What did Jesus do to the children once the apostles let them through?

Read Mark 10:16.

Little Man, Big Change

Luke 19:1–10

Hi, my name is Zacchaeus.

One day, everyone crowded the streets to see Jesus. I wanted to see Him, too. It's just that, well, er, I have a, um, *little* problem. My little problem is that I'm—you guessed it—short. I tried to see Him, but couldn't—even on my tippytoes! Then I got an idea!

I climbed a tree! I laugh every time I picture myself struggling up that tree! But it was the best "crazy" thing I've ever done because it let me meet Jesus!

Jesus noticed little ol' me! "Zacchaeus," He called up, "come down from there. Let's go to your house." I was stunned!

Jesus did something most people didn't—He *liked* me! I was a tax collector, see, and nobody liked tax collectors. "If I've cheated anybody," I announced, "I'll pay them back four times the amount!" Jesus smiled. "And I'm giving half of my things to the poor!" I added.

"Today," Jesus said, "salvation has come to this house!"

110

Who? Me?

Loving God should make you do "crazy" things, like share with others, overlook insults, and love people who hate you. Do something "nutty" for God today.

BIBLE VERSE

"But I say to you, love your enemies, bless those who curse you, do good to those who hate you, and pray for those who spitefully use you and persecute you, that you may be sons of your Father in heaven."
—Matthew 5:44–45

A big-shot little man

Zacchaeus was a *chief* tax collector. This means he held a superintendent or regional director position. Also, since Jericho was an important and productive city, he would've made even more money. The Bible tells us Zacchaeus was a wealthy man.

Did You Know?

The name Zacchaeus in Hebrew means *pure* or *righteous one*.

Challenge

What kind of tree did Zacchaeus climb?

Read Luke 19:4.

Jesus Cleans House

John 2:13–25; Matthew 21:12–13
Mark 11:15–17; Luke 19:45–46

Hey there, friend. It's me again, Peter.

We had such wonderful times with Jesus. We walked everywhere, so we had a lot of time to listen and learn from Him. Jesus didn't say one thing and do another. You could trust Jesus to be true to His word.

But, of course, you could also know a lot about Jesus by watching what He did. He spent hours talking, teaching, inspiring, and hugging people. He had compassion for people and helped them. He was also very passionate when it came to respecting God.

I'll never forget watching the time Jesus stormed through the temple during Passover. He was very angry to see how they had turned the temple into a marketplace. It looked more like a flea market than a house of God.

Jesus made a whip and ran them all out, knocking over their benches and tables as He did. "God's house is for prayer!" He shouted. "You've made it into a den of thieves!"

Who? Me?

Respect for God is at the top of Jesus' priorities. God isn't to be treated lightly, as a curse word, or ignored. God is to be worshiped, honored, praised, and obeyed. Make sure you always respect God with your words and actions.

BIBLE VERSE

"You shall walk after the LORD your God and fear Him, and keep His commandments and obey His voice; you shall serve Him and hold fast to Him."

—Deuteronomy 13:4

The treasured temple

Jesus told the prideful Pharisees that this "temple would be destroyed" and not a single stone would be left on top of another. In AD 70—only 40 years later—the armies of Rome did exactly what Jesus said they would.

Challenge

Find out what children were doing when Jesus was at the temple that day.

Read Matthew 21:15–16.

Did You Know?

A historian of that time named Josephus wrote that nearly 4 million people came to the Passover festivals in Jerusalem.

Dead Man Walking

John 11:1–44

Hi, my name is Mary.

One time my brother, Lazarus, was sick—really sick. I sent word to Jesus, "The one You love is sick."

"This illness," Jesus said, "will bring glory to God."

Then Lazarus died.

Jesus arrived after that. My sister, Martha, ran out to Him. "If You'd been here," she cried, "Lazarus would still be alive." Jesus told her, "Lazarus will rise again, Martha. I am the life and the resurrection. Do you believe in Me?" "Yes, Lord," Martha answered. "You are the Son of God."

We took Jesus to Lazarus's tomb. "Open it," Jesus told us. "But, Lord," Martha said, "Lazarus has been dead for four days now. It will stink." Then Jesus asked, "Didn't I say, if you believe, you will see the glory of God?" We moved the stone. Then He shouted, "Lazarus! Come out!"

And Lazarus did come out! Jesus brought my brother back to life!

Who? Me?

God doesn't always answer our prayers right away. God is good. God always does what is truly best and builds our faith up most. So keep believing!

BIBLE VERSE

Jesus said to him, "If you can believe, all things *are* possible to him who believes."

—*Mark 9:23*

A sweet-smelling gift

Mary, Martha, and Lazarus were good friends of Jesus. Once, at a dinner in Jesus' honor, Mary poured an expensive bottle of perfume on Jesus' feet and wiped them dry with her hair.

Read John 12:2–3.

Challenge

How much was the bottle of perfume worth?

Read John 12:5.

Did You Know?

Jesus knew that Lazarus had died before anyone told him.

Read John 11:11–15.

The King of Kings on a Cross

John 19:17–42; Matthew 27:27–66
Mark 15:16–47; Luke 23:26–55

Hi, I'm John.

I was a close friend of Jesus. I was also one of His disciples. I loved Him very much.

Jesus knew He was going to die. He told us about it the night it all began. After that solemn dinner, we went to a garden. Jesus prayed hard there. A crowd arrested Him and put Him on a cross to die. I stood by His mother, Mary, to comfort her. "Behold your son," Jesus told her. Then He looked at me. "Behold your mother." Mary lived with me from then on.

Then the sky turned dark right in the middle of the day. Jesus said, "It's finished." The earth shook, and the curtain in the temple ripped in two. "Father," Jesus called out, "into Your hands I commit My Spirit." Then He died.

One of the Roman soldiers who helped to crucify Jesus said, "Truly this was the Son of God!"

They took His body down, wrapped it in a linen cloth, and put Him in a tomb. Then, just to make sure no one could steal His body, they rolled a huge stone in front of the tomb.

Who? Me?

Jesus died for everyone—including the Roman soldier who didn't believe in Jesus until His death. God wants us to tell others what Jesus did because Jesus did it for them, too. Tell your friends about Jesus.

BIBLE VERSE

"For God so loved the world that He gave His only begotten Son, that whoever believes in Him should not perish but have everlasting life."

—*John 3:16*

Full of love till the very end

Even on the Cross, Jesus was full of love for His accusers. He forgave the thief who was on a cross beside Him; He made sure His mother would be looked after; and He asked God to forgive the mob of people who were killing Him and mocking Him, too.

Did You Know?

In Jesus' day, crucifixion was the most dishonorable death imaginable—used mostly for hated criminals.

Challenge

What sign did Pilate have put on the Cross of Jesus?

Read John 19:19–22.

117

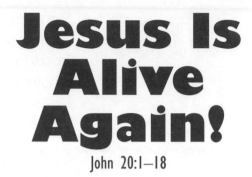

Jesus Is Alive Again!

John 20:1–18

Hi, my name is Mary Magdalene.

I was a close friend of Jesus. I went to His tomb so early it was still dark. I had to be close to Him. The stone had been rolled away from His tomb.

I ran to the disciples Peter and John. "They've taken our Lord!" I cried. "I don't know where they've put Him!" They rushed to see, but all they found were linen strips and the burial cloth. Then they went back to their homes.

I stayed and looked inside. I saw two angels sitting where Jesus' body had been. "Why are you crying?" they asked. "Because they've taken my Lord," I answered. "And I don't know where to find Him."

I turned around and saw a Man. I thought He was the gardener. "Do You know where they've taken Jesus?" I asked Him. "Mary," He said. It was Jesus! "Go," He said. "Tell My brothers I am going to My Father and your Father, to My God and your God."

I ran and told the disciples everything Jesus had said.

Who? Me?

Jesus' death was God's plan. It was why He came to earth. God has a plan for you, too. All you have to do is follow Him. Make sure you do what you know God wants you to do, and He will take care of the rest.

BIBLE VERSE

Your eyes saw my substance, being yet unformed. And in Your book they all were written, the days fashioned for me, when *as yet there were* none of them.

—*Psalm 139:16*

A friend to the end

Mary Magdalene was there when Jesus was put on trial; she was there when Pilate agreed to allow the people to crucify Jesus; and she saw Jesus being beaten and humiliated by the crowd. She stood close to Jesus during the crucifixion, hoping it would be of comfort to Him.

Did You Know?

Mary Magdalene wasn't really Mary Magdalene. Her name was actually Miriam. She was called Miriam of Magdala, because she was from a tiny fishing village called Magdala.

Challenge

How did Jesus help Miriam of Magdala?

Read Luke 8:1–3.

A Fishing Story

John 21:1–23

Hi, it's me—Peter.

I had decided to go fishing. "We'll go with you, Peter," a handful of other disciples said. So off we went. We fished all night but didn't catch any fish.

"Catch anything?" Someone shouted from the shore about 100 yards away. "Nope!" we answered. "Throw your net on the right side of the boat," He said. "You'll find some!" So we did, and the fish started filling our net!

"It's Jesus!" John said. I jumped into the water and swam to shore. "Have some breakfast," Jesus said. After breakfast, Jesus asked, "Do you love Me, Peter?"

"Yes, Lord. You know I do." He said, "Feed My lambs."

Then He asked me again. "Yes, Lord," I said. "You know I do." He said, "Tend My sheep."

Then He asked a third time. "Yes, Lord," I told Him, a little hurt. "You know I love You." He said, "Feed My sheep." And I did. I served fellow believers the rest of my life.

Who? Me?

Jesus wanted Peter to serve a community of believers who could help one another and the world. Jesus wants you to do the same. How? Just act like Jesus—serve others.

BIBLE VERSE

"For even the Son of Man did not come to be served, but to serve, and to give His life a ransom for many."

—*Mark 10:45*

The fishermen of Galilee

The Sea of Galilee is famous for its fish. There are 18 different species of fish found in it. The kind the disciples caught that morning were probably musht fish. These are large fish, some of which are 16 inches long and weigh 2 pounds.

Did You Know?

Nearly 500,000 people lived in Palestine during Jesus' lifetime.

Challenge

How many fish did the disciples catch?

Read John 21:11.

Come Back Soon, Jesus

Acts 1:1–11

Hey, it's me, Peter.

It had been a good while since Jesus was crucified and had come back to life. We learned so much from Him during this time. He taught us things about God and about God's kingdom and about the Scriptures.

Once again, we were having dinner with Jesus. "I've got a gift for each of you," He told us. "Stay in Jerusalem because that's where you're going to receive it. It's the Holy Spirit," He explained. "The Holy Spirit will give you power to teach people all over the world about God's kingdom."

Then—while we were looking right at Him—He went up in the sky. We stared while He disappeared above the clouds. "Why are you staring up there?" two angels asked us. "He'll come back some day, just like you've seen Him go."

Who? Me?

The Bible tells us that Jesus now sits at God's right side. Jesus, like a lawyer, pleads your case for you. Jesus understands all of your struggles, so you can be honest with God when you pray.

BIBLE VERSE

Therefore, in all things He had to be made like *His* brethren, that He might be a merciful and faithful High Priest in things *pertaining* to God, to make propitiation for the sins of the people.

—Hebrews 2:17

Where did this take place?

The Bible does not say it directly, but this event most likely happened on the Mount of Olives in Jerusalem.

Did You Know?

After His resurrection, Jesus appeared to more than 500 believers at the same time.

Read 1 Corinthians 15:6.

Challenge

Jesus appeared to the disciples over a period of how many days?

Read Acts 1:3.

Something's Up in the Upper Room

Acts 2:1–47

Hi there. It's me, Peter.

After Jesus went up to heaven, we waited in Jerusalem like He asked. Now, it was the Day of Pentecost. Thousands of people from all over the world filled the city.

Suddenly, we heard a sound like a furious windstorm coming from heaven. Then we saw tongues of fire resting on each one of us. We started speaking in languages we'd never learned.

People gathered outside our room. "Amazing!" they said. "What does this mean?" someone asked. "How is it that each of us is hearing them speak in our own native language?"

"Fellow Jews!" I shouted to the crowd. "This is what the prophet Joel said would happen!"

I told them about Jesus. Many felt deeply sorry. "What should we do now?" they asked. "Repent and be baptized," I explained, "so that your sins will be forgiven. And you will receive the gift of the Holy Spirit."

About 3,000 people did exactly that.

Who? Me?

It isn't easy to admit when you've done something wrong. But it's impossible to be free until you do. Admit your mistakes quickly. Don't lie to cover them up.

Spring harvest

Pentecost was also called the Feast of Weeks. It celebrated the first fruits of the early spring harvest. In Jesus' time, it had grown into a celebration of God's creation of His people and their religious history, too.

Did You Know?

The word pentecost means *fiftieth day*. Pentecost Sunday occurs 50 days following Easter Sunday.

Challenge

Memorize Acts 2:38.

Jumping for Jesus

Acts 3:1–26

Hi, my name is John.

I was one of Jesus' disciples. I was the first one to the tomb after Mary Magdala told us Jesus' body was missing. I loved Jesus very much.

After Jesus died, I told people about how Jesus loved them. Once Peter and I were walking to the temple. We saw a crippled man being carried to the temple gate to beg. He did this every day. "Please," he begged us. "Give me some money."

Peter and I looked straight at the man. "Look at us," Peter said. "We don't have any money, but we'll give you what we do have. In the name of Jesus Christ of Nazareth, walk."

Peter helped the man stand up. Instantly, the man's ankles and feet became strong. Many people knew this man and were astonished. "How can someone who is crippled walk?" they asked one another.

The man went with Peter and me into the temple. He was so excited he was leaping and jumping and praising God with all his energy.

126

Who? Me?

Can you imagine how this man's life was changed this day? If you can't, his joyful behavior would give you a good idea. Right? Can people see your thankfulness to God for all He's done (and does) for you? Let the world see that you're excited about Jesus.

BIBLE VERSE

"Let your light so shine before men, that they may see your good works and glorify your Father in heaven."

—*Matthew 5:16*

First steps

The Bible tells us this man had been crippled *since birth*. He had never been able to walk. These were his very first steps—and leaps!

Did You Know?

John was often called the apostle whom Jesus loved.

Challenge

What time of day was it?

Read Acts 3:1.

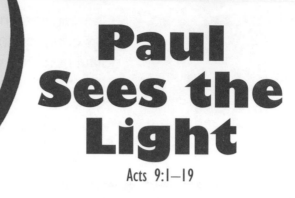

Paul Sees the Light

Acts 9:1—19

Hi, I'm Paul.*

I was a very religious man. When I learned that my religion was being threatened by followers of a dead troublemaker named Jesus, I did all I could to stop them.

One day a light from heaven flashed all around me. I fell to the ground. It was Jesus! "Saul, Saul!" He called to me. "Why are you hurting Me? Go into the city and wait." When I stood, I was blind.

Jesus appeared in a vision to another man. "Ananias," Jesus called. "Go to Judas's house. Ask for a man named Saul. He's praying." "But, Lord," Ananias said, "this man Saul is here to arrest Your followers." But the Lord said, "Go! I have chosen him to preach for Me now."

Ananias told me, "Brother Saul, the Lord Jesus, who appeared to you on the road, has sent me to you that you may see and be filled with the Holy Spirit."

Immediately, scalelike things fell from my eyes and I could see again. I was a changed man. I became a follower of Jesus. I taught people about Him till the day I died.

*Paul is the Roman name for Saul. After Saul believed in Jesus he was usually called Paul.

128

Who? Me?

Paul made a 180-degree turn. Got a bad attitude going? You can do a 180. Been avoiding prayer? Do a 180! Been a follower of bad things? Jesus will help you stop, turn around, and head in the right direction.

BIBLE VERSE

For godly sorrow produces repentance *leading* to salvation.

—*2 Corinthians 7:10*

A tough faith

Paul was struck 39 times with a whip on five different occasions; beaten with rods three times; stoned and left for dead once; shipwrecked three times; imprisoned for his faith; and, finally, he died a martyr's death for Jesus.

Did You Know?

Paul wrote 13 of the 27 books in the New Testament.

Challenge

What did Paul do to earn a living?

Read Acts 18:1–3.

Jailbreak

Acts 12:1–19

Hey again! It's me, Peter.

I was arrested for telling people about Jesus. While I was sleeping between the two guards I was chained to, an angel poked me in the side. "Wake up!" he said. "Get dressed!" And—*pling!*—just like that, the chains fell off my wrists. "Now," the angel said, "follow me."

We walked right past guards, through the city gate (which opened by itself!), and down the street. Then—*poof!*—the angel was gone. The Lord had saved me.

I went to Mary's house, where I knew folks were praying for me, and knocked on the door of the gate. Their servant Rhoda came to the door. She heard my voice and got so excited she ran back to the group and left me locked out! "Peter's at the door!" she told them. They said, "You're out of your mind!"

I kept knocking, and finally they let me in. We were all amazed at what God had done.

Who? Me?

God hears your prayers. Prayer works. Prayer changes things. Be patient with yourself—learning to pray takes practice. Start with one-minute prayers. Try one now.

BIBLE VERSE

"Therefore I say to you, whatever things you ask when you pray, believe that you receive *them*, and you will have *them*."

—*Mark 11:24*

Pray today

Praying is often not a natural, easy thing to do. Jesus' own disciples asked Him to teach them how to pray, because they didn't know how. So, don't get discouraged. Stay with it.

Did You Know?

Peter didn't know he was really escaping until the angel left him standing alone in the street. He thought he was having a vision.

Challenge

Memorize the Lord's Prayer.

See Matthew 6:9–13.

A Tough Trip

Acts 12:25–13:13; 15:36–41

Hello there. I am Barnabas.

Paul and I sailed from a town called Seleucia to a place called Cyprus, then to Salamis, where we preached in their synagogues. John Mark, my cousin, was our helper. We traveled through the whole island, then we sailed to Perga in Pamphylia. To our disappointment, John Mark left us and went back to Jerusalem.

Paul and I kept traveling. The Lord gave us power to do miraculous signs and wonders to show our message was true. Many people believed. Many didn't. Some ran us out of town. One group of people stoned Paul—then left him for dead—while another group called us gods. "We're just men," we told them sternly. "Worship God only!"

Some time later Paul said, "Let's go back to those towns, Barnabas, to see how they're doing." I wanted to take John Mark with us, too. "No!" Paul said. "John Mark deserted us last time." We got into a big argument about it. I ended up taking John Mark with me. Paul took Silas with him.

Years later, Paul asked for John Mark to help him again.

Who? Me?

Even the closest friends have disagreements. It's okay to disagree. It's not okay to turn disagreements into name-calling, bitterness, hatred, or violence. Control your anger. Do not let your anger control you.

BIBLE VERSE

"Be angry, and do not sin."

—*Ephesians 4:26*

Barnabas' life story

Barnabas was one of the first teachers in the early church in Antioch. His name was really Joseph, but the apostles called him Barnabas, which means *son of encouragement*. Barnabas was a friend to Paul when all the others were still afraid of him. Barnabas introduced Paul to the original apostles.

Did You Know?

Paul's missionary journeys covered close to 10,000 miles over a period of 20 years.

Challenge

Where were Jesus' followers first called Christians?

Read Acts 11:25–26.

Paul's Murder Prevented

Acts 23:1–31

Hi again. It's me, Paul.

I put many followers of Christ in prison, and I fully supported their being put to death. Now, after all these years of preaching *for* Jesus, I was the one who was in danger of being put to death for the very same reason.

Roman soldiers arrested me. They called all the religious leaders together. "Brothers," I told them, "I am a Pharisee. I'm on trial here because I believe in heaven." This caused a big argument because half of the group believed in heaven, too, and the other half did not. The argument was so bad the guards took me back to my cell so I'd be safe.

Then a group of men came up with a secret plan to kill me. "We'll kill him before he gets back to the trial," they said. My nephew heard them making the plan. "Tell the commander about this," I told him. And he did.

That night 200 soldiers, 70 horsemen, and another 200 spearmen took me away to another city in the middle of the night. I went to Rome after that. And everywhere I went, I told people about Jesus.

Who? Me?

Paul trusted God—even when things turned bleak. In happy times, in sad times, in good times, in bad times, always believe that God is there with you. Because He is.

Paul and Rome . . .

Paul was sent to Rome where he was in prison for two years. He continued to preach about Jesus. In 1941, an inscription was found indicating that during the time of Jesus there were more than four million people living in Rome.

Did You Know?

Paul went on *three* different missionary journeys.

You can read about them in Acts.

Challenge

How many men were in the group who planned to kill Paul?

Read Acts 23:13.

With my whole heart I have sought You;
Oh, let me not wander from Your commandments!
Your word I have hidden in my heart,
That I might not sin against You.

—Psalm 119:10–11